LEARN JAPANESE: COMMON WORDS IN CONTEXT

Explore the Japanese language

© **Copyright 2023 - All Rights Reserved.**

The content contained within this book may not be reproduced, duplicated or transmitted without direct written permission from the author or the publisher.
Under no circumstances will any blame or legal responsibility be held against the publisher, or author, for any damages, reparation, or monetary loss due to the information contained within this book, either directly or indirectly.

Legal Notice:

This book is copyright protected. It is only for personal use. You cannot amend, distribute, sell, use, quote or paraphrase any part, or the content within this book, without the consent of the author or publisher.

Disclaimer Notice:

Please note the information contained within this document is for educational and entertainment purposes only. All effort has been executed to present accurate, up-to-date, reliable, and complete information. No warranties of any kind are declared or implied. Readers acknowledge that the author is not engaged in the rendering of legal, financial, medical or professional advice. The content within this book has been derived from various sources. Please consult a licensed professional before attempting any techniques outlined in this book.

By reading this document, the reader agrees that under no circumstances is the author responsible for any losses, direct or indirect, that are incurred as a result of the use of the information contained within this document, including, but not limited to, errors, omissions, or inaccuracies.

Table of Contents

The Basics 11
Food 17
Verbs 22
Time 35
Common Adjectives 43
People 50
Expressing Feelings 57
Describing Things 68
At the bank 87
Places 104
Emotions 121
Daily Activities 130

こんにちは
KONNICHIWA

Whether you are a seasoned student of the Japanese language or a curious newcomer to its charms, use this guide as a companion on your linguistic journey.

Each chapter takes you through a selection of carefully selected words, and its practical usage.

How to Use this Guide:

For each word we've selected, we've provided the kanji where available, hiragana/katakana and the romaji translations to help you maximise your learning experience.

Here's an example:
1.
Word: I, (私), わたし, watashi
Grammar in context: Noun (common) (futsuumeishi)
Used in a sentence:
In kanji/hiragana/katakana: 私はハナです。
Romaji: Watashi wa Hana desu.
English translation: I am Hana.

If you are new to reading hiragana and katakana, you can use the reference charts in the following pages.

Note that each word will be used in a sentence with its romaji and English translations.

You may notice that in some scenarios (like the word shop), the same English word might repeat itself but there are multiple ways to describe a shop in Japanese.

If you have any questions at all, reach out to us on Instagram @LingoGeeks.

Best of luck with your learning journey!

Hiragana Chart

あ a	い i	う u	え e	お o
か ka	き ki	く ku	け ke	こ ko
さ sa	し shi	す su	せ se	そ so
た ta	ち chi	つ tsu	て te	と to
な na	に ni	ぬ nu	ね ne	の no
は ha	ひ hi	ふ fu	へ he	ほ ho
ま ma	み mi	む mu	め me	も mo
や ya		ゆ yu		よ yo
ら ra	り ri	る ru	れ re	ろ ro
わ wa		を wo		ん n

Katakana Chart

ア	a	イ	i	ウ	u	エ	e	オ	o
カ	ka	キ	ki	ク	ku	ケ	ke	コ	ko
サ	sa	シ	shi	ス	su	セ	se	ソ	so
タ	ta	チ	chi	ツ	tsu	テ	te	ト	to
ナ	na	ニ	ni	ヌ	nu	ネ	ne	ノ	no
ハ	ha	ヒ	hi	フ	fu	ヘ	he	ホ	ho
マ	ma	ミ	mi	ム	mu	メ	me	モ	mo
ヤ	ya			ユ	yu			ヨ	yo
ラ	ra	リ	ri	ル	ru	レ	re	ロ	ro
ワ	wa			ヲ	wo			ン	n

THE BASICS

1. I, (私), わたし, watashi

Noun (common) (futsuumeishi)

Used in a sentence:

私はハナです.

Watashi wa Hana desu.

I am Hana.

2. You, (貴方), あなた, anata

Noun (common) (futsuumeishi)

Used in a sentence:

あなたは、太郎です.

Anata wa Taro desu.

You are Taro.

3. They, (彼ら), かれら, karera

Noun (common) (futsuumeishi)

Used in a sentence:

彼らは、家族です.

Karera wa kazoku desu.

They are family.

4. We, 私たち, わたしたち, Watashitachi

Noun (common) (futsuumeishi)

Used in a sentence:

私たちは、友達です.

Watashitachi wa tomodachi desu.

We are friends.

5. This, これ, Kore

Noun (common) (futsuumeishi)

Uesd in a sentence:

これは、ペンです.

Kore wa pen desu.

This is a pen.

6. That, あれ, Are

Noun (common) (futsuumeishi)

Used in a sentence:

あれは、ケーキです.

Are wa cake desu.

That is a cake.

7. He, 彼, かれ, Kare

Noun (common) (futsuumeishi)

Used in a sentence:

彼は、私の弟です.

Kare wa watshino otouto desu.

He is my younger brother.

8. She, 彼女, かのじょ, Kanojo

Noun (common) (futsuumeishi)

Used in a sentence:

彼女は、私の先生です.

Kanojo wa watashi no sensei desu.

She is my teacher.

9. Ours, 私たちのもの, わたしたちのもの, Watashitach no mono

Noun (futsuumeishi)

Used in a sentence:

それは、私たちものです.

Sore wa watashitachi mono desu.

It is ours.

10. Yours, 貴方のもの, あなたのもの, Anartanomono

Noun (common) (futsuumeishi)

Used in a sentence:

この自転車は、貴方のものです。

Kono jitensya wa anatanomono desu.

This bike is yours.

FOOD

11. Eat, 食べる, たべる, Taberu

Verb (common)

Used in a sentence:

私は、うどんを食べます.

Watashi wa udon wo tabemasu.

I eat Udon.

12. Drink, 飲む, のむ, Nomu

Verb (common)

Used in a sentence:

私は、緑茶を飲みます.

Watashi wa ryokucya wo nomimasu.

I drink green tea.

13. Cook, 料理をする, りょうりをする, Ryori wo suru

Verb (common)

Used in a sentence:

私は、カレーを料理します.

Watashi wa kare wo ryori shimasu.

I cook curry and rice.

14. Sweet, 甘い, あまい, Amai

Adjective (common)

Used in a sentence:

この果物は、甘いです。

Kono kudamono wa amai desu.

This fruit is sweet.

15. Sour, 酸っぱい, すっぱい, Suppai

Adjective (common)

Used in a sentence:

このスープは酸っぱいです。

Kono su-pu wa suppai desu.

This soup is sour.

16. Spicy, 辛い, からい, Karai

Adjective (common)

Used in a sentence:

韓国料理は辛いです。

Kankoku ryori wa karai desu.

Korean dishes are spicy.

17. Eat in, 店内で, 店内で, Tennaide

Vocabulary (common)

Used in a sentence:

私は店内で食べます.

Watashi wa tennaide tabemasu.

I eat in store.

18. Takeaway, 持ち帰り, もちかえり, Mochikaeru

Noun (common)

Used in a sentence:

これは、持ち帰り用のピザです.

Korewa mochikaeri youno pizza desu.

This is a takeaway pizza.

COMMON VERBS

19. To do, する, Suru

Verb (common)

Used in a sentence:

私は、毎日宿題をします．

Watashi wa mainichi shukudai wo shimasu.

I do homework every day.

20. To make, 作る, つくる, Tsukuru

Verb (common)

Used in a sentence:

太郎は、家を作ります．

Taro wa ie wo tsukurimasu.

Taro makes houses.

21. To go, 行く, いく, Iku

Verb (common)

Used in a sentence:

私たちは、午後に、東京スカイツリーに行きます．

Watashitachi wa gogoni, Tokyo Skytree ni ikimasu.

We are going to Tokyo Skytree this afternoon.

22. To use, 使う, つかう, Tsukau

Verb (common)

Used in a sentence:

私は、スマートフォンを5年以上使っています.

Watashiwa smaerohone wo go nen izyou tsukatteimasu.

I have been using my smartphone for over 5 years.

23. To have, 持つ, もつ, Motsu

Verb (common)

Used in a sentence:

彼女は、ルイヴィトンのバックを持っています.

Kanojo wa Luis Vitton no bakku wo motteimasu.

She has a Louis Vuitton bag.

24. To buy, 買う, かう, Kau

Verb (common)

Used in a sentence:

私のお母さんは、寿司を毎週金曜日に買います.

Watashino okasan wa sushi wo maisyuu kinnyoubi ni kaimasu.

My mother buys sushi every Friday.

25. To be given, 貰う, もらう, Morau

Verb (common)

Used in a sentence:

私は、私の彼氏から指輪を貰いました.

Watashi wa watashino kareshi kara yubiwa wo moraimashita.

I was given a ring by my boyfriend.

26. To think, 思う, おもう, Omou

Verb (common)

Used in a sentence:

私は、東京に引っ越そうと思います.

Watashi wa Tokyo ni hikkkosouto omoimasu.

I think that I will move to Tokyo.

27. To see, 見る, みる, Miru

Verb (common)

Used in a sentence:

彼らは、美しい景色を見ます.

Karera wa utsukushii keshiki wo mimasu.

They see a beautiful view.

28. To hear, 聞く, きく, Kiku

Verb (common)

Used in a sentence:

私は、あなたが言ったことが聞こえませんでした.

Watashi wa anataga ittakoto ga kikoemasenndeshita.

I didn't hear what you said.

29. To speak, 話す, はなす, Hanasu

Verb (common)

Used in a sentence:

私は、日本語を話します.

Watashi wa nihongo wo hanashimasu.

I speak Japanese.

30. To know, 知る, しる, Shiru

Verb (common)

Used in a sentence:

彼が何て言ったか知っていますか?

Kare ga nante ittaka shitteimasuka?

Do you know what he said?

31. To become, なる, Naru

Verb (common)

Used in a sentence:

彼女は医者になりたいです

Kanojo wa isya ni naritaidesu

She wants to become a doctor.

32. To say, tell, 伝える, つたえる, Tsutaeru

Verb (common)

Used in a sentence:

私はあなたに日本について話しましょう.

Watashi wa anatani nihon ni tsuite hanashimasyou.

I will tell you about Japan.

33. To study, 勉強する, べんきょうする, Benkyou suru

Verb (common)

Used in a sentence:

私は、瞑想について勉強します.

Watashi wa meisou ni tsuite benkyou shimasu.

I study meditation.

34. To wake, 起きる, おきる, Okiru

Verb (common)

Used in a sentence:

いつも何時に起きますか?

Itsumo nanji ni okimasuka?

What time do you usually wake up?

35. To understand, 理解する, りかいする, Rikaisuru

Verb (common)

Used in a sentence:

私は、あなたのことを理解します。

Watashi wa anata no kotowo rikai shimasu.

I understand you.

36. To take, 連れて行く, つれていく, Tsurete iku

Verb (common)

Used in a sentence:

私の両親は、今年の冬にオーストラリアに私を連れていきます。

Watashino ryoushin wa kotoshi no fuyu ni australia ni watashi wo tsurete ikimasu.

My parents will take me to Australia this winter.

37. To sell, 売る, うる, Uru

Verb (common)

Used in a sentence:

リンゴは、一個５ドルで売られています。

Ringo wa ikko go doru de urareteiru.

They sell apples at five dollars each.

38. To teach, 教える, おしえる, Oshieru

Verb (common)

Used in a sentence:

私の母は、生け花を教えています。

Watashi no haha wa ikebana wo oshiete imasu.

My mother teaches flower arranging.

 The fastest way to learn a new language is to fully immerse yourself in it. Try to speak Japanese with others who are trying to learn, watch Japanese movies with subtitles or listen to Japanese music when you can.

39. To pay, 払う, はらう, Harau

Verb (common)

Used in a sentence:

私は、家賃を毎月払います．

Watashi wa maitsuki yachin wo haraimasu.

I pay rent every month.

40. To memorize, 覚える, おぼえる, Oboeru

Verb (common)

Used in a sentence:

トモコは、歌を覚えることがとても得意です．

Tomoko wa uta wo oboeru kotoga totemo tokui desu.

Tomoko is really good at memorizing songs.

41. To forget, 忘れる, わすれる, Wasureru

Verb (common)

Used in a sentence:

私は、家の鍵をよく家の中に忘れる．

Watashi wa ie no kagi wo yoku wasureru.

I often forget my keys at home.

42. To sit, 座る, すわる, Suwaru

Verb (common)

Used in a sentence:

座って下さい

Suwatte kudasai.

Please sit down.

43. To walk, 歩く, あるく, Aruku

Verb (common)

Used in a sentence:

私の祖母は毎日1時間歩きます.

Watashino sobo wa mainichi ichijikan arukumasu.

My grandmother walks for 1 hour every day.

44. To raise/lift, 持ち上げる, もちあげる, Mochiageru

Verb (common)

Used in a sentence:

私は、簡単に重い箱を持ち上げることができます.

Watashi wa kantan ni omoi hako wo mochiageru kotoga dekimasu.

 I can lift heavy boxes easily.

45. To draw/pull, 引く, ひく, Hiku

Verb (common)

Used in a sentence: 彼女の美しさが彼の注意を引いた

Kanojo no utsukushisa ga kare no cyui wo hiita.

Her beauty drew his attention.

46. To sleep, 寝る, ねる, Neru

Verb (common)

Used in a sentence:

私の子供は夜の8時に寝ます

Watashino kodomo wa yoruno hachiji ni nemasu

My kid sleeps at 8 pm.

47. To rest, 休む, やすむ, Yasumu

Verb (common)

Used in a sentence:

あなたは、少し休んだ方が良いです.

Anata wa sukoshi yasunda houga yoi desu.

You should get some rest.

48. To sing, 歌う, うたう, Utau

Verb (common)

Used in a sentence:

マイコは歌うことが好きです。

Maiko wa utau kotoga sukidesu.

Maiko likes to sing a song.

TIME

49. Now, 今, いま, Ima

Adverb (common)

Used in a sentence:

もう行かなくてはいけません

Mou ikanakuteha ikemasen

I have to leave now.

50. Time, 時間, じかん, Jikan

Adverb (common)

Used in a sentence:

時間が経つのは早いですね

Jikan ga sugirunoowa hayai desune.

Time flies.

51. Later, 後で, あとで, Atode

Adverb (common)

Used in a sentence:

また後で会いましょう. Mata atode aimasyou.

I will see you later.

52. Then, その時, そのとき, Sonotoki

Adverb (common)

Used in a sentence:

ちょうどその時、バスが止まりました

Cyoudo sonotoki basu ga tomarimashita, ust then.

The bus stopped.

53. Start, 始める, はじめる, Hajimeru

Verb(common)

Used in a sentence:

私は、最近新しい趣味でテニスを始めました.

Watashi wa saikin atarashii syumi de tennis wo hajimemashita.

I started a new hobby which is tennis recently.

54. Finish, 終わる, おわる, Owaru

Verb (common)

:Used in a sentence:

あなたは、仕事が終わりましたか?

Anata wa shigoto ga owarimashitaka?

Are you finished with your work?

55. Often, よく, Yoku

Adverb (common)

Used in a sentence:

私はよく寝言を言います。

Watashi wa yoku negoto wo iimasu.

I talk in my sleep very often.

56. Morning, 朝, あさ, Asa

Noun (common)

Used in a sentence: 私は朝、ヨガをします, Watashi wa asa Yoga wo shimasu.

I do yoga in the morning.

57. Afternoon, 午後, ごご, Gogo

Noun (common)

Used in a sentence: 私は、午後買い物に行きます。

Watashi wa gogo kaimono ni ikimasu.

 I go shopping in the afternoon.

58. Evening, 夜, よる, Yoru

Noun (common)

Used in a sentence:

はい、とても素敵な夜ですね.

Hai totemo sutekina yoru desune.

Yes, it's such a nice evening.

59. When, 〜の時, no toki

Adverb (common)

Used in a sentence:

私が子供の時、公園で遊んでいた

Watashi ga kodomo no toki, kouen de asonde ita.

When I was a kid, I played in the park.

60. Before, 前, まえ, Mae

Adverb (common)

Used in a sentence:

仕事に行く前に、朝ご飯を食べます

Shigoto ni ikumaeni asagohan wo tabemasu.

Before I go to work, I eat breakfast.

61. After, 後, あと, Ato

Adverb (common)

Used in a sentence:

ジムに行った後、シャワーを浴びます

Gym ni itta ato shower wo abimasu.

After I went to the gym, I take a shower.

62. Seldom, めったに〜ない, Mettani ___ nai

Adverb (common)

Used in a sentence:

私は、めったに怒らない.

Watashi wa mettani okoranai.

I seldom get angry.

63. Early, 早く, はやく, Hayaku

Adverb (common)

Used in a sentence: 私は早く学校に行きます.

Watashi wa hayakui kimasu.

 I go to school early.

64. Late, 遅い, おそい, Osoi

Adverb (common)

Used in a sentence:

私は、昨日遅く寝た.

Watashi wa kinou osoku neta.

I went to bed late at night.

65. Slow, ゆっくり, Yukkuri

Adverb (common)

Used in a sentence:

私は、ゆっくりとした生活を送りたいです.

Watashi wa yukkuri toshita seikatsu wo okuritai desu.

I want to have a slow life.

66. Fast, 速く, はやく, Hayaku

Adverb (common)

Used in a sentence:

私は速く走ることができます.

Watashi wa hayaku hashiru kotoga dekimasu.

I can run fast.

COMMON ADJECTIVES

67. Tall, 高い, たかい, Takai

Adjective (common)

Used in a sentence:

私の父は、背が高いです．

Watashi no chichi wa sega takaidesu.

My father is tall.

68. Short, 短い, みじかい, Mijikai

Adjective (common)

Used in a sentence:

少しの間ここに滞在します．

Sukoshi no aida koko ni taizai shiamsu.

I will stay here for a short period.

69. Small, 小さい, ちいさい, Chiisai

Adjective (common)

Used in a sentence:

私の犬は小さくて可愛いです．

Watashi no inu wa chiisakute kawaii desu.

 My dog is small and cute.

70. Big, 大きい, おおきい

Adjective (common)

Used in a sentence:

私の友達の家はとても大きいです.

Watashino tomodachi no ie wa totemo ookiidesu.

My friend's house is very big.

71. Long, 長い, ながい, Nagai

Adjective (common)

Used in a sentence:

あの川は長いです.

Ano kawa wa nagai desu.

That river is long.

72. Few, 少し, すこし, Sukoshi

Adverb (common)

Used in a sentence:

彼女は、友達が少しはいます.

Kanojo wa tomodachi ga sukoshi wa imasu.

She has a few friends.

73. Little, 少し, すこし, Sukoshi

Adverb (common)

Used in a sentence:

私は少し時間があります.

Watashiwa sukoshi jikan ga arimasu.

I have a little time.

74. A lot, 沢山, たくさん, Takusan

Adverb (common)

Used in a sentence:

私は、沢山食べます.

Watashi wa takusan tabemasu.

I eat a lot.

75. Many, 沢山, たくさん, Takusan

Adverb (common)

Used in a sentence:

日本には、美しい場所が沢山あります.

Nihon niwa utsukushii basyo ga takusan arimasu.

There are many beautiful places in Japan.

76. Heavy, 重い, おもい, Omoi

Adjective (common)

Used in a sentence:

この重い荷物を運ぶのを手伝ってくれませんか?

Kono omoi nimotsu wo hakobu nowo tetsudatte kuremasennka?,

Please help me with this heavy baggage.

77. Light, 軽い, かるい, Karui

Adjective (common)

Used in a sentence:

私は軽い靴が好きです.

Watashi wa karui kutsu ga sukidesu.

I like light shoes.

78. Near, 近い, ちかい, Chikai

Preposition (common)

Used in a sentence:

家の近くにレストランがあります.

Ie no chikaku ni restaurant ga arimasu.

There is a restaurant near my house.

70. Far, 遠い, とおい, Tooi

Preposition (common)

Used in a sentence: 私の職場はアパートから遠いです.

Watashi no syokuba wa apart kara tooi desu.

My office is far from my apartment.

PEOPLE

80. Who, 誰, だれ, Dare

Question word (common)

Used in a sentence:

あなたは誰ですか?

Anata wa dare desuka?

Who are you?

81. Doctor, 医者, いしゃ, Isya

Noun (common)

Used in a sentence:

私の従兄弟は医者です.

Watashi no itoko wa isya desu.

My cousin is a doctor.

82. Teacher, 先生, せんせい, Sensei

Noun (common)

Used in a sentence:

私の先生はとても優しいです.

 Watashi no sensei wa totemo yasashii desu.

My teacher is very kind.

83. Student, 生徒, せいと, Seito

Noun (common)

Used in a sentence:

私の中学校は生徒が200人います.

Watashi no chugakkou wa seito ga nihyaku-nin imasu.

There are 200 students in my junior high school.

84. Girlfriend, 彼女, かのじょ, Kanojo

Noun (common)

Used in a sentence:

私の彼女は旅行が好きです.

Watashi no kanojo wa ryokou ga sukidesu.

My girlfriend like to travel.

85. Boyfriend, 彼氏, かれし, Kareshi

Noun (common)

Used in a sentence:

私は、彼氏と1ヶ月前に別れてしまいました.

Watashi wa kareshi to ikkagetsu maeni wakarete shimaimashita,

I broke up with my boyfriend about a month ago

86. Daughter, 娘, むすめ, Musume

Noun (common)

Used in a sentence:

私の娘はもうすぐ2歳になります．

Watashino musume wa mousugu nisai ni narimasu.

My daughter will be 2 years old soon.

87. Son, 息子, むすこ, Musuko

Noun (common)

Used in a sentence:

私の息子は、サッカー選手です．

Watashi no musuko wa soccer player desu.

My son is a soccer player.

88. Mom, お母さん, おかあさん, Okasan

Noun (common)

Used in a sentence:

私のお母さんは、オーストラリア出身です．

Watashi no okasan wa australia shushhin desu.

My mom is from Australia.

89. Dad, お父さん, おとうさん, Otousan

Noun (common)

Used in a sentence:

私のお父さんは、会社を経営しています.

 Watashino otousan wa kaisya wo keiei shiteimasu.

 My dad runs his own business.

90. Cousin, 従兄弟, いとこ, Itoko

Noun (common)

Used in a sentence:

私の従兄弟は、とても頭が良いです.

Watashi no itoko wa totemo atama ga yoi desu.

 My cousin is very smart.

91. Child, 子供, こども, Kodomo

Noun (common)

Used in a sentence:

私の子供はとても可愛いです.

Watashi no kodomo wa totemo kawaii desu.

 My child is very cute.

92. Baby, 赤ちゃん, あかちゃん, Akachan

Noun (common)

Used in a sentence:

赤ちゃんは大体、一日で沢山昼寝をします.

Akachan wa daitai ichinichi de takusan hirune wo shimasu.

Babies usually nap a lot in a day.

93. Friend, 友達, ともだち, Tomodachi

Noun (common)

Used in a sentence:

私は３年ぶりに友達に会いました.

Watashi wa sannen buri ni tomodachi ni aimashita.

I met a friend I hadn't seen for three years.

94. Everybody, 皆んな, みんな, Minna

Noun (common)

Used in a sentence:

皆んな、音楽が大好きです.

Minna, ongaku ga daisuki desu.

Everybody loves music.

EXPRESSING FEELINGS

95. Like, 好き, すき, Suki

Verb (common)

Used in a sentence:

私は、彼が好きだと思います.

Watashi wa kare ga suki dato omoimasu.

I think I like him.

96. Love, 大好き, だいすき, Daisuki

Verb (common)

Used in a sentence:

私は、日本のアニメが大好きです.

Watashi wa nihon no anime ga daisuki desu.

I love Japanese anime.

97. Dislike, 嫌う, きらう, Kirau

Verb (common)

Used in a sentence:

沢山の生徒が数学が嫌いです.

Takusan no seito ga suugaku ga kiraidesu.

Many students dislike math.

98. Love, 大好き, だいすき, Daisuki

Verb (common)

Used in a sentence:

私は、日本のアニメが大好きです．

Watashi wa nihon no anime ga daisuki desu.

 I love Japanese anime.

99. Hate, 大嫌い, だいきらい, Daikirai

Verb (common)

Used in a sentence:

私は、野菜が大嫌いです．

Watashi wa yasai ga daikirai desu.

 I hate vegetables.

100. Enjoy, 楽しむ, たのしむ, Tanoshimu

Verb (common)

Used in a sentence:

私は、本を読むことを楽しみます．

Watashi wa hon wo yomu koto wo tanoshimi masu.

 I enjoy reading a book.

101. Happy, 幸せ, しあわせ, Shiawase

Adjective (common)

Used in a sentence:

私は、とても幸せです.

Watashi wa totemo shiawase desu.

I am very happy.

102. Sad, 悲しい, かなしい, Kanashi

Adjective (common)

Used in a sentence:

何がそんなに悲しいの.

Naniga sonnani kanashii no?.

What makes you so sad?

103. Excited, わくわくする, Wakuwaku suru

Adjective (common)

Used in a sentence:

私は、東京に行くことがわくわくします.

Watashi wa Tokyo ni ikukoto ga wakuwaku shimasu.

I am excited to go to Tokyo.

104. Embarrassed, 恥ずかしい, はずかしい, Hazukashii

Adjective (common)

Used in a sentence:

私は、人前でスピーチをすることが恥ずかしいです.

Watashi wa hitomae de speech wo surukotoga hazukashii desu,

I was embarrassed to do a speech in front of people.

105. Feelings, 感情, かんじょう, Kanjo

Noun (common)

Used in a sentence:

私は、彼の感情が分かりません.

Watashi wa kare no kanjo ga wakarimasen.

I can't understand his feelings.

106. Shy, 内気の,うちきの, Uchikino

Adjective (common)

Used in a sentence:

私は、内気です.

Watashi wa uchiki desu.

I am shy.

DESCRIBING THINGS

107. New, 新しい, あたらしい, Atarashii

Adjective (common)

Used in a sentence:

これは、新しい車です.

Korewa atarashii kuruma desu.

This is a new car.

108. Old, 古い, ふるい, Furui

Adjective (common)

Used in a sentence:

この服は、古いです.

Korewa no fuku wa furui desu.

These clothes are old.

109. Thick (books), 厚い, あつい, Atsui

Adjective (common)

Used in a sentence:

この本は厚いです.

Kono hon wa atsui desu.

This book is thick.

110. Thin, 薄い, うすい, usui

Adjective (common)

Used in a sentence:

この紙は、薄いです.

Kono kami wa usui desu.

This paper is thin.

111. Hot (weather), 暑い, あつい, Atsui,

Adjective (common)

Used in a sentence:

今日は、とても暑いです.

Kyou wa totemo atsui desu.

It is very hot today.

112. Cold / Chilly (weather), 寒い, さむい, samui

Adjective (common)

Used in a sentence:

アイスランドは、寒い国です.

Aisurando wa samui kuni desu.

Iceland is a cold country.

113. Warm (weather), 暖かい, あたたかい, Atatakai

Adjective (common)

Used in a sentence:

私は、暖かい天気が好きです.

Watashi wa atatakai tenki ga suki desu.

I like warm weather.

114. Cool (weather), 涼しい, すずしい, Suzushii,

Adjective (common)

Used in a sentence:

レストランの中は、いつも涼しい.

Restaurant no naka wa itsumo suzushii.

It is always cool in the restaurant.

115. Hot (drink), 熱い, あつい, atsui

Adjective (common)

Used in a sentence:

私は、熱いコーヒーを注文します.

Watashi wa atsui coffee wo cyumon shimasu.

I will order a hot coffee.

116. Cold (drink), 冷たい, つめたい, tsumetai

Adjective (common)

Used in a sentence:

私は、冷たいビールが好きです.

Watashi wa tsumetai bi-ru ga suki desu.

I like cold beer.

117. Warm (drink), 温かい, あたたかい, atatakai

Adjective (common)

Used in a sentence:

私は、温かい白湯を朝飲みます.

Watashi wa atatakai sayu wo nomimasu.

I drink warm water in the morning.

118. Interesting, 面白い, おもしろい, omoshiroi

Adjective (common)

Used in a sentence:

この小説は、面白いです.

Kono syousetsu wa omoshiroi desu.

This novel is interesting.

119. Dull / Boring, 詰まらない, つまらない, tsumaranai

Adjective (common)

Used in a sentence:

このイベントは、つまらないです.

Kono event wa tsumaranai desu.

This event is boring.

120. Wide, 広い, ひろい, hiroi

Adjective (common)

Used in a sentence:

北海道は、広いです.

Hokkaido wa hiroi desu.

Hokkaido is wide.

121. Narrow, 狭い, せまい, semai

Adjective (common)

Used in a sentence:

この道は、狭いです.

Kono michi wa semai desu.

This road is narrow.

122. Expensive, 高い, たかい, takai

Adjective (common)

Used in a sentence:

最近、果物が高いです.

Saikin, kudamono ga takai desu.

Fruit is expensive recently.

123. Cheap, 安い, やすい, yasui

Adjective (common)

Used in a sentence:

日本の寿司は、安いです.

Nihon no sushi wa yasui desu.

Sushi in Japan is cheap.

123. Fat/Thick, 太い, ふとい, futoi

Adjective (common)

Used in a sentence:

私の父は、太っている.

Watashi no chichi wa futotte iru.

My father is fat.

124. Thin / Slender / Narrow, 細い, ほそい, hosoi

Adjective (common)

Used in a sentence:

モデルは、細いです.

Moderu wa hosoi desu.

Fashion models are slender.

125. Tasty, 美味しい, おいしい, oishii

Adjective (common)

Used in a sentence:

日本食は、美味しいです.

Nihon syoku wa oishii desu.

Japanese foods are tasty.

126. Unappetizing / Tasteless, 不味い, まずい, mazui

Adjective (common)

Used in a sentence:

野菜は、不味いです.

Yasai wa mazui desu.

Vegetables are tasteless.

127. Difficult, 難しい, むずかしい, muzukashii

Adjective (common)

Used in a sentence:

日本語は、難しいです。

Nihongo wa muzukashii desu.

Japanese is difficult.

128. Easy / Simple, 易しい, やさしい, yasashii

Adjective (common)

Used in a sentence:

英語は、易しいです。

Eigo wa yasashii desu.

English is easy.

129. Good / Nice / OK / Prefer, 良い, いい / よい, ii / yoi

Adjective (common)

Used in sentence:

運動をすることは、良いことです。

Undou wo surukoto wa yoi koto desu.

Doing exercise is good.

130. Easy / Simple, 易しい, やさしい, yasashii

Adjective (common)

Used in a sentence:

英語は、易しいです.

Eigo wa yasashii desu.

English is easy.

131. Good / Nice / OK / Prefer, 良い, いい / よい, ii / yoi

Adjective (common)

Used in sentence:

運動をすることは、良いことです.

Undou wo surukoto wa yoi koto desu.

Doing exercise is good.

132. Bad / Wicked, 悪い, わるい, warui

Adjective (common)

Used in a sentence:

夜遅くまで起きていることは、悪いです.

Yoru okokumade okiteiru koto wa warui desu.

Staying up too late is bad.

133. Cute / Pretty, 可愛い, かわいい, kawaii

Adjective (common)

Used in a sentence:

私の猫は、とても可愛いです.

Watashino neko wa totemo kawaii desu.

My cat is very cute.

134. Red, 赤い, あかい, akai

Adjective (common)

Used in a sentence:

机の上に赤い果物があります.

Tsukue no ue ni akai kudamono ga arimasu.

There is red fruit on the desk.

135. Blue, 青い, あおい, aoi

Adjective (common)

Used in a sentence:

私は、青い空が好きです.

Watashi wa aoi sora ga suki desu.

 I like blue skies.

136. White, 白い, しろい, shiroi

Adjective (common)

Used in a sentence:

長野では、沢山白い雪が降ります。

Nagano dewa takusan shiroi yuki ga hurimasu.

There is a lot of white snow in Nagano

137. Black, 黒い, くろい, kuroi

Adjective (common)

Used in a sentence:

私は、黒い服を沢山持っています。

Watashi wa kuroi fuku wo takusan motte imasu.

I have a lot of black clothes.

138. Round, 丸い, まるい, marui

Adjective (common)

Used in a sentence:

メロンは、丸いです。

Melon wa marui desu.

Melons are round.

139. Hard, 固い, かたい, katai

Adjective (common)

Used in a sentence:

煎餅は固いです。

Senbei wa katai desu.

Rice crackers are hard.

140. Soft, 柔らかい, やわらかい, yawarakai

Adjective (common)

Used in a sentence:

あなたの手は、柔らかいです。

Anatano te wa yawarakai desu.

You have soft hands.

141. Bright / Light, 明るい, あかるい, akarui

Adjective (common)

Used in a sentence:

月は、明るいです。

Tsuki wa akarui desu.

The moon is bright

142. Dark / Gloomy, 暗い, くらい, kurai

Adjective (common)

Used in a sentence:

雨の日は、少し暗いです.

Ameno hi wa sukoshi kurai desu.

It is a little dark when it is rainy.

143. Busy, 忙しい, いそがしい, isogashii

Adjective (common)

Used in a sentence:

私は、忙しいです.

Watashi wa isogashii desu.

I am busy.

144. Beautiful / Clean, 綺麗, きれい (*), kirei

Adjective (common)

Used in a sentence:

京都は、綺麗です.

Kyoto wa kirei desu.

Kyoto is beautiful.

145. Dirty, 汚い, きたない, kitanai

Adjective (common)

Used in a sentence:

私の兄の部屋は、汚いです.

Watashi no ani no heya wa kitanai desu.

My older brother's room is dirty.

146. Sleepy, 眠い, ねむい, nemui

Adjective (common)

Used in a sentence:

私は、昼食の後眠くなります.

Watashi wa cyusyoku no ato nemuku narimasu.

I feel sleepy after lunch.

147. Young, 若い, わかい, wakai

Adjective (common)

Used in a sentence:

私の母は、若く見えます.

Watashino haha wa wakaku miemasu.

My mother looks young.

148. Strong / Tough, 強い, つよい, tsuyoi

Adjective (common)

Used in a sentence:

私は、メンタルが強いです．

Watashi wa mental ga tsuyoi desu.

I have strong mental health.

149. Weak, 弱い, よわい, yowai

Adjective (common)

Used in a sentence:

彼女の身体は、弱すぎます．

Kanojo no karada wa yowasugi masu.

She is too weak.

150. Painful, 痛い, いたい, itai

Adjective (common)

Used in a sentence:

蜂に刺されるととても痛いです．

Hachi ni sasareruto totemo itai desu.

 Bee stings can be very painful.

151. Correct / Right, 正しい, ただしい, tadashii

Adjective (common)

Used in a sentence:

彼は、正しいです。

Kare wa tadashii desu.

He is right.

152. Lively / Bustling / Busy, 賑やか, にぎやか, nigiyaka

Adjective (common)

Used in a sentence:

音楽フェスティバルは、賑やかです。

Ongaku festival wa nigiyaka desu.

The music festival is lively.

153. Quiet, 静か, しずか, shizuka

Adjective (common)

Used in a sentence:

私の近所は、静かです。

Watashi no kinjo wa shizuka desu.

My neighbor is quiet.

154. Strong / Robust / Healthy, 丈夫, じょうぶ, joubu

Adjective (common)

Used in a sentence:

私の彼氏は、丈夫です。

Watashi no kareshi wa jobu desu.

My boyfriend is strong.

155. Various, 色々, いろいろ, iroiro

Adjective (common)

Used in a sentence:

私は、色々な音楽が好きです。

Watashi wa, iroiro na ongaku ga sukidesu.

I like various types of music.

156. Kind, 親切, しんせつ, shinsetsu

Adjective (common)

Used in a sentence:

彼女は、優しいです。

Knojo wa yasahii desu.

She is kind.

157. Healthy / Vigorous / Energetic, 元気, げんき, genki

Adjective (common)

Used in a sentence:

子供たちは、元気です.

Kodomo tachi wa genki desu.

Children are energetic.

158. Convenient, 便利, べんり, benri

Adjective (common)

Used in a sentence:

日本の交通は、便利です.

Nihon no koutsuu wa benri desu.

Transportation in Japan is convenient.

159. Complicated, 複雑, ふくざつ, fukuzatsu

Adjective (common)

Used in a sentence:

日本語の文法は、複雑です.

Nihon go no bunpou wa fukuzatsu desu.

Japanese grammar is complicated.

160. Free (time), 暇, ひま, hima

Noun (common)

Used in a sentence:

私は、今週の日曜日は暇です。

Konsyu no nichiyoubi wa hima desu.

I am free this Sunday.

161. Skillfull / Good at, 上手, じょうず, jouzu

Noun (common)

Used in a sentence:

彼は、サッカーが上手です。

Kare wa soccer ga jouzu desu.

He is good at soccer.

162. Unskillful / Poor at, 下手, へた, heta

Noun (common)

Used in a sentence:

私は、ピアノが下手です。

Watashi wa piano ga heta desu.

I am poor at playing piano.

163. Fresh, 新鮮, しんせん, shinsen

Noun (common)

Used in a sentence:

この野菜は、新鮮です.

Kono yasai wa shinsen desu.

This vegetable is flesh.

164. Wonderful / Lovely / Cool, 素敵, すてき, suteki

Noun (common)

Used in a sentence:

あなたは、素敵ですね.

Anata wa suteki desune.

You are lovely.

165. All Right / No Problem, 大丈夫, だいじょうぶ, daijoubu

Noun (common)

Used in a sentence:

大丈夫だよ。上手くいくから.

Daijoubu dayo. Umaku ikukara.

All right. It is going to be okay.

166. Polite, 丁寧, ていねい, teinei

Noun (common)

Used in a sentence:

彼らは、丁寧です.

Karera wa teinei desu.

They are polite.

167. Famous, 有名, ゆうめい (*), yuumei

Noun (common)

Used in a sentence:

彼らのグループは、有名です.

Karera no group wa yuumei desu.

Their group is famous.

168. Strange / Odd, 変, へん, hen

Noun (common)

Used in a sentence:

近所の人は、変です.

Kinjo no hito wa hen desu.

My neighbor is strange.

169. Regrettable / Sorry / Pity, 残念, ざんねん, zannen

Noun (common)

Used in a sentence:

友達のお母さんが亡くなって、残念に思います.

Tomodachi no okasan ga naku natte, zannen ni omoimasu.

I feel sorry for my friend who lost his mother.

170. Safe, 安全, あんぜん, anzen

Noun (common)

Used in a sentence:

この地域は安全です.

Kono chiki wa anzen desu.

This area is safe.

AT THE BANK

171. Bank, 銀行, ぎんこう, ginkou

Noun (common)

Used in a sentence:

私は、新しく銀行の口座を開設しなければいけません．

Watashi wa ginkou no kouza wo kaisetsushinakereba ikemasen,

I have to open a bank account.

172. Bank Staff, 銀行員, ぎんこういん, ginkouin

Noun (common)

Used in a sentence:

私のお父さんは、銀行員です．

Watashi no otousan wa ginkouin desu.

My father is a bank staff.

173. Information Desk, 受付, うけつけ, uketsuke

Noun (common)

Used in a sentence:

私は、道に迷ったので受付に行きます．

Watashi wa michi ni mayotta node uketsuke ni ikimasu.

I will go to the information desk because I got lost.

174. Information Desk, 受付, うけつけ, uketsuke

Noun (common)

Used in a sentence:

私は、道に迷ったので受付に行きます．

Watashi wa michi ni mayotta node uketsuke ni ikimasu.

I will go to the information desk because I got lost.

175. Teller Window, 窓口, まどぐち, madoguchi

Noun (common)

Used in a sentence:

携帯が故障したので、窓口に聞こう．

Keitai ga kosyou shitanode madoguchi ni kikou.

Let's ask a teller because my phone is broken.

176. Numbered ticker, 番号札, ばんごうふだ, bangou fuda

Noun (common)

Used in a sentence:

もう少しで番号札で呼ばれます。

Mousukoshi de bangou fuda de yobare masu.

They will call your numbered ticket in a moment.

177. Safe, 金庫, きんこ, kinko

Noun (common)

Used in a sentence:

私の家には、金庫があります.

Watashino ie niwa kinko ga arimasu.

 My house has a safe.

178. Safe-Deposit Box, 貸金庫, かしきんこ, kashi kinko

Noun (common)

Used in a sentence:

あなたは、貸金庫があると言っていました.

Anata wa kashi kinko ga aruto itte ishimashita.

You said you had a safety deposit box.

179. Personal Seal, 判子, はんこ, hanko

Noun (common)

Used in a sentence:

あなたは、判子を持ってきましたか?

Anata wa kanko wo motte kimashitaka?

Did you bring your personal seal?

180. Personal Seal, 印鑑, いんかん, inkan

Noun (common)

Used in a sentence: 印鑑は、公的文書では必要です, Inkan wa kouteki bunsyo dewa hitsuyou desu, Personal Seal is needed for official document.

181. Municipal Office / City Hall , 市役所, しやくしょ, shiyakusho

Noun (common)

Used in a sentence:

市役所がどこにあるか知っていますか?

Shiyakusyo ga doko ni aruka shitteimasuka?

Do you know where a city hall is?

182. Bank Account, 口座, こうざ, kouza

Noun (common)

Used in a sentence:

あなたは、口座を開設しましたか?

Anatawa kouza wo kaisetsu shimashita ka?.

Did you open your bank account?

183. Bank Account Number, 口座番号, こうざばんごう, kouza bangou

Noun (common)

Used in a sentence:

あなたの口座番号は何ですか?

Anata no kouza bangou wa nandesuka?

What is your Bank Account Number?

184. Cash Card / ATM Card, キャッシュカード, kyasshu ka-do

Noun (common)

Used in a sentence:

キャッシュカードは、便利です.

Kyasshu ka-do wa benri desu.

Cash cards are very useful.

185. IC Card, IC カード, IC ka-do,

Noun (common)

Used in a sentence:

私は、ICカードで昼食を買いました.

Watashi wa IC card de cyusyoku wo kaimashita.

I bought my lunch with IC card.

186. Cash Dispenser / Automatic Teller Machine, キャッシュディスペンサー, kyasshu disupensa-

Noun (common)

Used in a sentence:

あなたは、キャッシュディスペンサーをどのコンビニでも見つけられます。

Anata wa kyasshu disupensa- wo dono konbini demo mitsukeraremasu.

You can find Cash Dispensers in any convenience store.

187. ATM, エーティーエム, e-ti-emu

Noun (common)

Used in a sentence:

ATMはどこですか？

E-ti-emu wa dokodesuka?

Do you know where the ATM is?

188. PIN / Password Number, 暗証番号, あんしょうばんごう, anshou bangou

Noun (common)

Used in a sentence:

あなたの暗証番号は何ですか？

Anata no anshou bangou wa nandesuka?

What is your PIN?

189. Deposit, 預金, よきん, yokin

Noun (common)

Used in a sentence:

いくら預金額がありますか？

Ikura yokin ga arimasuka?

How much deposit do you have?

190. Remittance, 送金, そうきん, soukin

Noun (common)

Used in a sentence:

すみませんが，身分証明書がないと送金されたお金は受け取れません，

Sumimasennga, mibunsyoumeisyo ga naito soukin sareta okane wa uketoremasen,

I'm sorry, but without an I.D. you cannot receive a remittance.

191. National Health Insurance Card, 国民健康保険証, こくみんけんこうほけんしょう, kokumin kenkou hokenshou

Noun (common)

Used in a sentence:

日本に住むときは、国民健康保険証が必要です. Nihon ni sumu toki wa, Kokumin Kenkō Hokenshō ga hitsuyō desu.

When you live in Japan, you will need a National Health Insurance Card.

192. Loan, 貸金 かしきん, kashikin

noun (common)

Used in a sentence:

あなたは、貸金がありますか?

Anata wa kashikin ga arimasuka?

Do you have a loan?

193. Loan, ローン, ro-n

Noun (common)

Used in a sentence:

私は、家を購入したのでローンがあります.

Watashi wa ie wo kounyu shitanode ro-n ga arimasu.

I bought a house, so I have a loan.

194. Debt, 借金 しゃっきん, shakkin

Noun (common)

Used in a sentence:

私の父は、借金があります.

Watashino chichi wa shakkin ga arimasu.

My father has debt.

195. Repayment, 返済 へんさい, hensai

Noun (common)

Used in a sentence:

毎月５万円の返済額を支払うのは大変です．

Maitsuki go manen no hensai gaku wo shiharaunowa taihen desu. It's hard to meet the monthly repayments of 50,000 yen.

196. Cash Withdrawal, 引き出し ひきだし, hikidashi

Noun (common)

Used in a sentence:

私はお金を引き出します．

Watashi wa okane wo hikidashi masu.

I'll make a cash withdrawal.

197. Cash Deposit, 預け入れ あずけいれ, azukeire

Noun (common)

Used in a sentence:

私の母は、預け入れが沢山あります．

Watashino haha wa azukeire ga takusan arimasu.

My mother has a lot of cash deposits.

198. Payment made via Bank Deposit Transfer , 振込 ふりこみ, furikomi

Noun (common)

Used in a sentence:

私は今日、ATMに振り込みにいかないといけません.

Watashi wa kyou ATM ni furikomi ni ikanaito ikemasen.

I have to go to ATM for a payment made via bank deposit transfer.

199. Transfer money from one account to another, 振替, ふりかえ, furikae

Noun (common)

Used in a sentence:

私は、振替で送金をします.

Watashi wa furikae de soukin wo shimasu.

I transfer money from one account to another.

200. Balance, 残高, ざんだか, zandaka

Noun (common)

Used in a sentence:

残高はいくらありますか?

Zandaka wa ikura arimasuka?

How much do you have in your balance?

201. Balance Inquiry, 残高照会 ざんだかしょうかい, zandaka shoukai
Noun (common)
Used in a sentence:
日本の全てのATMは残高照会の機能があります.
Nihon no subete no ATM wa zandaka syoukau no kinou ga arimasu.
Every Japanese ATM has a function of balance inquiry.

202. 記帳 きちょう, kichou Entry, Registration
Noun (common)
Used in a sentence:
私は通帳に記帳をしました.
Watashi wa tsucyou ni kicyou wo shimashita.
I made the entries in the bankbook.

203. Passbook / Bankbook, 通帳 つうちょう, tsuuchou noun
Noun (common)
Used in a sentence:
あなたは、通帳を持ってきましたか?
Anata wa tsucyou wo motte kimashitaka?
Did you bring your bankbook?

204. Passbook Update, 通帳更新, つうちょうこうしん, tsuuchou koushin

Noun (common)

Used in a sentence:

最近いつ通帳更新しましたか？

Saikin itsu tsucyou koushin shimashitaka?

When did you do a passbook update recently?

205. Paper Money / Bill / Note, 紙幣, しへい, shihei

Noun (common)

Used in a sentence:

私は、沢山の国の紙幣をもっています．

Watashi wa takusan no kuni no shihei wo motteimasu.

I have a lot of paper money from many counties.

206. Coin / Hard Money, 硬貨 こうか, kouka

Noun (common)

Used in a sentence:

私は、硬貨を集めることが好きです．

Watashi wa kouka wo atsumeru kotoga sukidesu.

I like to collect coins.

207. Money Exchange, 両替 りょうがえ, ryougae

Noun (common)

Used in a sentence:

両替のカウンターはどこですか?

Ryougae no kaunta- wa dokodesuka?

Where is the money exchange counter?

208. Foreign Money Exchange, 外貨両替, がいかりょうがえ, gaika ryougae

Noun (common)

Used in a sentence:

ここで外貨両替ができますか?

Kokode gaika ryougae ga dekimasuka?

Can I exchange money here?

209. Service Charge / Commission, 手数料, てすうりょう tesuuryou

Noun (common)

Used in a sentence:

手数料はいくらですか?

Tesuuryou wa ikura deuska?

How much will the service charge be?

210. Bank Transfer Fee, 振込手数料, ふりこみてすうりょう, furikomi tesuuryou

Noun (common)

Used in a sentence:

ここは、振込手数料が高いです.

Kokowa furikomi tesuuryou ga takaidesu.

The bank transfer fee is expensive here.

211. Payment Form, 振込用紙 ふりこみようし, furikomi youshi

Noun (common)

Used in a sentence:

振り込み用紙に記入しましたか?

Furikomi youshi ni kinyuu shimashitaka?

Did you fill in the payment form?

212. Dollar, ドル, doru

Noun (common)

Used in a sentence:

現在、1ドルは145円です.

Genzai ichi doru wa hyakuyonju go en desu.

A dollar is 145 yen now.

213. Euro ユーロ yu-ro

Noun (common)

Used in a sentence:

ユーロは円よりも強いです.

Yu-ro wa en yori mo tsuyoi desu.

Euro is stronger than Yen.

214. Yen 円 えん en

Noun (common)

Used in a sentence:

お昼ご飯は1000円でした.

Ohirugohan wa sen en deshita.

I spent 1000 yen on lunch today.

215. Shop / Store 店 みせ mise

Noun (common)

Used in a sentence:

私の家の近くには、店が沢山あります.

Watashi no ie no chikaku niwa mise ga takusan arimasu.

There are a lot of shops near my house.

PLACES

216. Shop / Store, 商店, しょうてん, shou ten

Noun (common)

Used in a sentence:

商店は、商品が安いです.

Syouten wa syouhin ga yasui desu.

It is cheaper to buy products in this shop.

217. Long-established Shop, 老舗 しにせ, shinise

Noun (common)

Used in a sentence:

ここは老舗です.

 Koko wa shinise desu.

Here is a long-established shop.

218. Beauty Salon / Hairdresser's Salon, 美容院, びよういん, biyou in

Noun (common)

Used in a sentence:

最近、いつ美容院に行きましたか?

Saikin, itsu biyou in ni ikimashita ka?

When did you go to a beauty salon recently?

219. Hair Salon, 理容室 ,りようしつ, riyou shitsu

Noun (common)

Used in a sentence:

美容院と理容室、どちらが好きですか?

Biyou in to riyou shitsu dochiraga suki desuka?

Which one do you prefer, a beauty salon or a hair salon?

220. Barbershop / Barber, 床屋, とこや, tokoya

Noun (common)

Used in sentence:

男性は、よく床屋に行きます.

Dansei wa yoku tokoya ni ikimasu.

Men often go to barber.

221. Barbershop, 理髪店, りはつてん, rihatsu ten

Noun (common)

Used in a sentence:

私は、めったに理髪店に行きません.

Watashi wa metta ni rihatsu ten ni ikimasen.

I rarely go to a barbershop.

222. Stationery Shop / Stationery, 文房具店 ,ぶんぼうぐてん, bunbou gu ten

Noun (common)

Used in a sentence:

私は、鉛筆を買うために文房具店に行きます.

Watashi wa enpitsu wo kau tame ni bunbou gu ten ni ikimasu.

I go to a stationery shop to buy pencils.

223. Department Store デパート depa-to

Noun (common)

Used in a sentence:

今週の日曜日、デパートに行きましょう.

Konsyu no nichiyoubi depa-to ni ikimasyou.

Let's go to a department store this Sunday.

224. Supermarket, スーパー ,su-pa-

Noun (common)

Used in a sentence:

私は、スーパーで沢山の野菜を買います.

Watashi wa su-pa- de takusan no yasai wo kaimasu.

I buy a lot of vegetables in the supermarket.

225. Greengrocer / Vegetable Shop, 八百屋 やおや, yao ya

Noun (common)

Used in a sentence:

私の市には、八百屋はありません.

Watashi no shi ni wa yao ya wa arimasen.

My city doesn't have vegetable shops.

226. Grocery Store, 乾物屋, かんぶつや, kanbutsu ya

Noun (common)

Used in a sentence:

食料雑貨が販売される市場です.

Shokuryou zakka ga hanbai sareteiru ichiba desu.

A marketplace is where groceries are sold.

227. Butcher / Meat Shop, 肉屋 に,くや, niku ya

Noun (common)

Used in a sentence:

私は、肉屋のステーキが好きです.

Watashi wa niku ya no sute-ki ga sukidesu.

I like the steaks in a meat shop.

228. Fish Dealer / Fishmonger, 魚屋 ,さかなや, sakana ya

Noun (common)

Used in a sentence:

魚屋には、沢山の新鮮な魚が売っています.

Sakana ya ni wa takusan no shinsen na sakana ga utte imasu.

There is a lot of fresh fish at a fish dealer.

229. Liquor Store, 酒屋, さかや, saka ya

Noun (common)

Used in a sentence:

私は、ビールを買いに酒屋に行きます.

Watashi wa bi-ru wo kaini saka ya ni ikimasu.

 I go to a liquor store to buy beers.

230. Japanese-style Bar, 居酒屋, いざかや, izaka ya

Noun (common)

Used in a sentence:

居酒屋は、沢山の食べ物と飲み物があり楽しいです.

Izakaya wa takusan no tabemono to nomimono ga ari tanoshiidesu.

I enjoy eating and drinking in Japanese-style bars.

231. Bar, バー, ba-

Noun (common)

Used in a sentence:

私は、バーの雰囲気が好きです。

Watashi wa bar no funiki ga sukidesu.

I like the atmosphere at the bar.

232. Florist, 花屋 ,はなや, hana ya

Noun (common)

Used in a sentence:

私は、お母さんの誕生日には花屋で花を買います。

Watashi wa okasan no tanjoubi ni wa hana ya de hana wo kaimasu.

I buy flowers from a florist on my mom's birthday.

233. Bookstore / Bookshop, 本屋 , ほんや ,hon ya

Noun (common)

Used in a sentence:

私は、今日本屋に行く予定です。

Watashi wa kyou hon ya ni iku yotei desu.

I am going to a bookstore today.

234. Bookstore / Bookshop, 書店, しょてん, sho ten

Noun (common)

Used in a sentence:

私は、新しい辞書を買いに書店に行きます．

Watashi wa atarashi jisyo wo kaini sho ten ni ikimasu.

 go to a bookstore to get a new dictionary.

235. Pharmacy, 薬屋, くすりや, kusuri ya

Noun (common)

Used in a sentence:

私は、熱があるので薬屋に行かないと行けません．

Watashi wa netsu ga arunode kururi ya ni ikanaito ikemasen.

I had to go to the pharmacy because I have a fever.

236. Pharmacy / Drugstore, 薬局, やっきょく, yakkyoku

Noun (common)

Used in a sentence:

病院に行った後は、薬局で薬を買います．

Byouin ni itta ato wa yakkyoku de kururi wo kaimasu.

I always get medicines after I go to a clinic.

237. Drugstore / Pharmacy, ドラッグストア, doraggu sutoa

Noun (common)

Used in a sentence:

ドラッグストアには、野菜も日用品も売っています.

Dotaggu sutoa niwa yasai mo nichiyouhin mo utteimasu.

Drugstores have vegetables and daily-use items, too.

238. Bakery, パン屋, ぱんや pan ya

Noun (common)

Used in a sentence:

私は、パン屋に毎週末行きます.

Watashi wa panya ni maishu matsu ikimasu

I go to the bakery every weekend.

239. Fruit Store, 果物屋, くだものや, kuda mono ya

Noun (common)

Used in a sentence:

果物屋の果物は、いつも新鮮で甘いです.

Kuda mono ya no kuda mono wa itsumo shinsen de amai desu

Fruit in fruit stores are always fresh and sweet.

240. Sushi Restaurant, 寿司屋, すしや, sushi ya

Noun (common)

Used in a sentence:

寿司屋では、手で食べる方が美味しいです.

Sushi ya dewa te de taberu hou ga oishii desu.

It is better to use your hands when you go to a sushi restaurant.

241. Pawnshop, 質屋, しちや, shichi ya

Noun (common)

Used in a sentence:

私は、アクセサリーを売りに質屋に行く予定です.

Watashi wa akusesari- wo uri ni shichi ya ni iku yotei desu.

I am going to go to a pawnshop to sell my accessories.

242. Wholesale Store 問屋 とんや ton ya

Noun (common)

Used in a sentence:

商品を問屋で買う方が安いです.

Syouhin wo ton ya de kau hou ga yasui desu.

It is cheaper to buy products at a wholesale store.

243. Shoe Store / Shoemaker, 靴屋, くつや, kutsu ya

Noun (common)

Used in a sentence:

私は、靴屋で新しい靴を買いました.

Watashi wa kutsu ya de atarashi kutsu wo kaimashita.

I bought new shoes at shoe store.

244. Bicycle Shop, 自転車屋, じてんしゃや, jitensha ya

Noun (common)

Used in a sentence:

私の自転車が壊れてしまったので自転車屋で直してもらいます.

Watashi no jitensha ga kowarete shimatta node jitensya wo naoshite moraimasu.

My bicycle was broken, so I will go to a bicycle shop to fix it.

245. Toy Shop, 玩具屋, おもちゃや, omocha ya

Noun (common)

Used in a sentence:

私が子供の時、よく玩具屋に行きました.

Watashi ga kodomo no toki yoku omocha ya ni ikimashita.

I used to go to a toy shop a lot when I was a child.

246. Furniture Store, 家具屋 ,かぐや, kagu ya

Noun (common)

Used in a sentence:

私は、新しい市に引っ越したので家具屋に行きたいです.

Watashi wa atarashii shi ni hikkoshitanode kagu ya ni ikitai desu.

I want to go to a furniture store because I moved to a new city.

247. Electric Appliance Store, 電気屋, でんきや, denki ya

Noun (common)

Used in a sentence:

この地域で、一番近くの電気屋はどこですか?

Kono chiiki de ichiban chikaku no denki ya wa doko desuka?

Where is the nearest electric appliance store in this area?

248. Cleaning Store / Dry Cleaning Shop, クリーニング屋 クリーニングや, kuri-ningu ya

Noun (common)

Used in sentence:

私のお母さんは、クリーニング屋で働いています.

Watashi no okasan wa kuri-ningu ya de hataraite imasu.

My mother works at a cleaning store.

249. Locksmith, 錠前屋, じょうまえや, joumae ya

Noun (common)

Used in a sentence:

私は、家の鍵を無くしたので錠前屋に行かなければいけません。

Watashi wa ie no kagi wo nakushite shimatta node joumae ya ni ikanakereba ikemasen.

I lost my house key, so I have to go to a locksmith.

250. Clothes Store, 洋品店, ようひんてん ,youhin ten

Noun (common)

Used in a sentence: 明日、一緒に洋品店に行きませんか？

Asu issyoni youhin ten ni ikimasenka?

Shall we go to a clothes store together tomorrow?

251. Coffee Shop / Coffee Lounge / Cafe, 喫茶店, きっさてん, kissa ten

Noun (common)

Used in a sentence:

私は、いつも喫茶店で勉強をします。

Watashi wa itsumo kissa ten de benkyou wo shimasu

I always study at a cafe.

252. Chinese Restaurant, 中華料理店, ちゅうかりょうりてん, chuuka ryouri ten

Noun (common)

Used in a sentence:

今夜、中華料理屋に行きませんか?

Konya chuuka ryouri ten ni ikimasenka?

Can we go to a Chinese restaurant tonight?

253. Cafeteria / Dining Hall, 食堂, しょくどう, shoku dou

Noun (common)

Used in a sentence:

私は、よく食堂で昼ご飯を食べます.

Watashi wa yoku shoku dou de hirugohan wo tabemasu.

I often eat my lunch at the cafeteria.

254. Restaurant, レストラン, resutoran

Noun (common)

Used in a sentence:

あなたは、どのレストランが好きですか?

Anata wa dono resutoran ga sukidesuka?

Which restaurants do you like to go?

255. Convenience Store, コンビニ, konbini

Noun (common)

Used in a sentence:

日本のコンビニには、色々な食べ物や飲み物が売っています.

Nihon no konbini niwa iroiro na tabemono ya nomimono ga utteimasu.

Japanese convenience stores have a lot of foods and drinks

256. Pet Shop, ペットショップ, petto shoppu

Noun (common)

Used in a sentence:

日本には、まだペットショップが沢山あります.

Nihon niwa mada petto shoppu ga takusan arimasu.

There are still many pet shops in Japan.

257. Movie Theater / Cinema, 映画館, えいがかん, eiga kan

Noun (common)

Used in a sentence:

私は、毎週金曜日に映画館に行きます.

Watashi wa maishu kinyoubi ni eiga kan ni ikimasu.

I go to a movie theater every Friday.

258. Photo Studio, 写真館, しゃしんかん, shashin kan

Noun (common)

Used in a sentence:

私は、写真館で結婚式の写真を撮りました．

Watashi wa shashin kan de kekkon shiki no shashin wo torimashita.

I took pictures for my wedding at a photo studio.

EMOTIONS

259. to be surprised, 驚く, おどろく, odoroku

Verb (common)

Used in a sentence:

私は、驚きました.

Watashi wa odoroki mashita.

I was surprised.

260. cry, 泣く, なく, naku

Verb (common)

Used in a sentence:

子供は、公園で泣いていました.

Kodomo wa kouen de naite imashita.

A kid was crying in the park.

261. get angry, 怒る, おこる, okoru

Verb (common)

Used in a sentence:

私のお母さんは、私に怒っています.

Watashi no okasan wa watashi ni okotte imasu.

My mother got angry at me.

262. laugh, 笑う, わらう, warau

Verb (common)

Used in a sentence:

彼女は笑っていました.

Kanojo wa watte imashita.

She was laughing.

263. fear, 怖がる, こわがる, kowagaru

Verb (common)

Used in a sentence:

彼はその危険を恐れなかった.

Kare wa sono kiken wo osorena katta.

He didn't fear the danger.

264. fall in love, 惚れる, ほれる, horeru

Verb (common)

Used in a sentence:

私は、あなたに惚れました.

Watashi wa anata ni horemashita.

I fell in love with you.

265. panic, be flustered, 慌てる, あわてる, awateru

Verb (common)

Used in a sentence:

私は慌てました.

Watashi wa awate mashita.

I was panicked.

266. comfort, console, 慰める, なぐさめる, nagusameru

Verb (common)

Used in a sentence:

彼女は悲しんでいる私を慰めてくれました.

Kanojo wa kanashinde iru watashi wo nagusamete kuremashita

She comforted me in my grief.

267. think, 思う, おもう, omou

Verb (common)

Used in a sentence:

私は、あなたが正しいと思います.

Watashi wa anataga tadashii to omoimasu.

I think you are right.

268. consider, 考える, かんがえる, kangaeru

Verb (common)

Used in a sentence:

あなたは、良く考えた方が良いです。

Anata wa yoku kangaeta houga yoi desu.

I think you should consider it well.

269. praise, 褒める, ほめる, homeru

Verb (common)

Used in a sentence:

私たちは彼のすばらしい演奏をほめました。

Watashi tachi wa kare no subarashii ensou wo homemashita.

We praised him for his wonderful performance.

270. support, 支える, ささえる, sasaeru

Verb (common)

Used in a sentence:

私は、私の夫を支えます。

Watashi wa watashino otto wo sasaemasu.

I will support my husband.

271. get tired, 疲れる, つかれる, tsukareru

Verb (common)

Used in a sentence:

私は、今日はとても疲れました。

Watashi wa kyou wa totemo tsukaremashita.

I got so tired today.

272. suffer, 苦しむ, くるしむ, kurushimu

Verb (common)

Used in a sentence:

あなたは、苦しまなくてよいです。

Anata wa kurushima nakute yoi desu.

You don't have to suffer.

273. become hurt, damaged, 痛む, いたむ, itamu

Verb (common)

Used in a sentence:

背中が痛いです。

Senaka ga itai desu.

My back hurts.

274. to believe, 信じる, しんじる, shinjiru

Verb (common)

Used in a sentence:

彼は、あなたを信じています.

Kare wa anata wo shinjite imasu.

He believes in you.

275. to need, 必要, ひつよう, hitsuyou

Verb (common)

Used in a sentence:

私は、スーパーに行く必要があります.

Watashi wa su-pa- ni iku hitsuyou ga arimasu.

I need to go to the supermarket today.

276. make a mistake, 間違える, まちがえる, machigaeru

Verb (common)

Used in a sentence:

私は、間違えてしまいました.

Watashi wa machigaete shimaimashita.

I made a mistake.

278. love, be affectionate, 可愛がる, かわいがる, kawaigaru

Verb (common)

Used in a sentence:

私の父は、私の子供たちを可愛がります.

Watashi no chichi wa watashi no kodomo wo kawaigari masu.

My dad loves my kids.

DAILY ACTIVITIES

279. to live, 住む, すむ, sumu

Verb (common)

Used in a sentence:

私は、沖縄に住んでいます.

Watashi wa okinawa ni sunde imasu

I live in Okinawa.

280. to wash, 洗う, あらう, arau

Verb (common)

Used in a sentence:

私は、食器を洗います.

Watashi wa shokki wo arai masu.

I wash plates.

281. to turn on (light), 付ける, つける, tsukeru

Verb (common)

Used in a sentence:

私は、電気を付けました.

Watashi wa denki wo tsuke mashita.

I turned on the light.

282. to return (home), 帰る, かえる, kaeru

Verb (common)

Used in a sentence:

私は、日本に帰ります.

Watashi wa nihon ni kaerimasu.

I return to Japan.

283. to cut, 切る, きる, kiru

Verb (common)

Used in a sentence:

私は、野菜を切ります.

Watashi wa yasai wo kirimasu.

I cut vegetables.

284. help, 手伝う, てつだう, tetsudau

Verb (common)

Used in a sentence:

私は、お母さんを手伝います.

Watashi wa okasan wo tetsudai masu.

I help my mom.

285. brush (teeth), 磨く, みがく, migaku

Verb (common)

Used in a sentence:

私は、歯を磨きます。

Watashi wa ha wo migakimasu.

I brush my teeth.

私は、歯を磨きます。

286. to bring , 持ってくる, もってくる, mottekuru

Verb (common)

Used in a sentence:

私は、箱を持ってきま.

Watashi wa hako wo mottekimasu.

I'll bring a box.

287. to smoke, タバコを吸う, た ばこをすう, tabakowo suu

Verb (common)

Used in a sentence:

私のお父さんはタバコを吸っています。

Watashi no otousan wa tabako wo sutteimasu.

My dad smokes cigarettes.

www.ingramcontent.com/pod-product-compliance
Lightning Source LLC
Chambersburg PA
CBHW070308010526
44107CB00056B/2525